anythink

D1442290

Fire Salamanders

Sam Hesper

PowerKiDS press™

New York

Published in 2015 by The Rosen Publishing Group, Inc.
29 East 21st Street, New York, NY 10010

First Edition

Editor: Caitie McAneney
Book Design: Michael J. Flynn

Photo Credits: Cover Raimund Linke/Photolibrary/Getty Images; p. 5 Marek R. Swadzba/Shutterstock.com; p. 6 Erni/Shutterstock.com; p. 7 Matt Jeppson/Shutterstock.com; p. 9 hfuchs/Shutterstock.com; p. 11 Andreas Zerndl/Shutterstock.com; p. 12 juniart/Shutterstock.com; pp. 13, 21 Berndt Fischer/Photographer's Choice/Getty Images; p. 15 (coral snake) Patrick K. Cambell/Shutterstock.com; p. 15 (poison dart frog) Dirk Ercken/Shutterstock.com; p. 17 Vova Shevchuk/Shutterstock.com; p. 19 James Gerholdt/Shutterstock.com; p. 20 Eric Isselee/Shutterstock.com; p. 22 Vitalii Hulai/Shutterstock.com.

Library of Congress Cataloging-in-Publication Data

Hesper, Sam.
Fire salamanders / by Sam Hesper.
p. cm. — (Animal cannibals)
Includes index.
ISBN 978-1-4777-5764-2 (pbk.)
ISBN 978-1-4777-5749-9 (6-pack)
ISBN 978-1-4777-5761-1 (library binding)
1. Salamanders — Juvenile literature. I. Hesper, Sam. II. Title.
QL668.C2 H47 2015
597.8—d23

Manufactured in the United States of America

CPSIA Compliance Information: Batch #CW15PK: For Further Information contact Rosen Publishing, New York, New York at 1-800-237-9932

Contents

Slimy Salamanders

Have you ever seen a salamander? These slimy critters can be found both on land and in water. There are many kinds of salamanders, and they all have features that set them apart. The fire salamander has a black body and yellow markings, while the red salamander has a red body and black markings.

What do all salamanders have in common? Salamanders are **amphibians**. They're cold-blooded, which means their body heat depends on their surroundings. Salamanders look small, but they're actually predators. The fearsome fire salamander is also a cannibal. That means it eats its own kind!

FOOD FOR THOUGHT

What's the difference between amphibians and **reptiles**? Most reptiles have scales and lay eggs with hard shells on land. Most amphibians have smooth skin and lay soft eggs in water.

Some people think a salamander looks like a lizard and a toad put together. What do you think?

Different Species

Scientists have discovered about 600 species, or types, of salamanders around the world. Each species has certain features that set it apart from other species. Some salamander species are newts, which are salamanders that spend most of their life on land. Others are called sirens, which are salamanders that can breathe underwater and don't have back legs because they mostly swim.

The axolotl salamander is one species being studied by scientists. Why? Because if it loses a leg or tail, it will grow back!

FOOD FOR THOUGHT

Fire salamanders aren't the only cannibal salamander species. The tiger salamander is known to take a bite out of its own kind, too!

The largest land-living salamander is the barred tiger salamander. Like fire salamanders, tiger salamanders are usually black and yellow. Tiger salamanders live in North America and grow to 14 inches (36 cm) long.

Fire Salamander Bodies

Like most salamanders, fire salamanders have four short legs and a long tail. Fire salamanders use their tail to help them balance when walking on land. Fire salamanders have a large mouth, sharp teeth, and a sticky tongue that's good for catching tasty insects.

You can tell a fire salamander apart from other salamanders by looking at its coloring. Most fire salamanders are black with bright yellow markings. Some fire salamanders have markings that are orange or red instead of yellow. The markings are spots or stripes. What do you think a fire salamander's body feels like?

FOOD FOR THOUGHT

Fire salamanders grow to be about 8 inches (20 cm) long.

Fire salamanders stay moist, which means they're slimy and wet. That can help you tell it apart from lizards, which are scaly and dry.

Where Do They Live?

There are 13 kinds of fire salamanders around the world. Each one is called a subspecies because it's a type of fire salamander, which is a type of salamander. While you can find salamanders all over the world, fire salamanders are found only in the Eastern **Hemisphere**. Fire salamanders live mostly in central and southern Europe. You can also find them in parts of the Middle East and northern Africa.

It's actually hard to find fire salamanders. That's because they're noctural. That means they're active at night, when most people and animals are sleeping.

It's also hard to find fire salamanders because, like other salamanders, they spend most of their time hiding under things.

Keeping Cool

Many ancient people thought fire salamanders lived in fire. That's because when they lit a fire, fire salamanders came out of the logs. The salamanders were actually escaping from their burning homes!

During hot summers, some fire salamanders hide underground in a deep sleep to avoid the heat. That's called estivation.

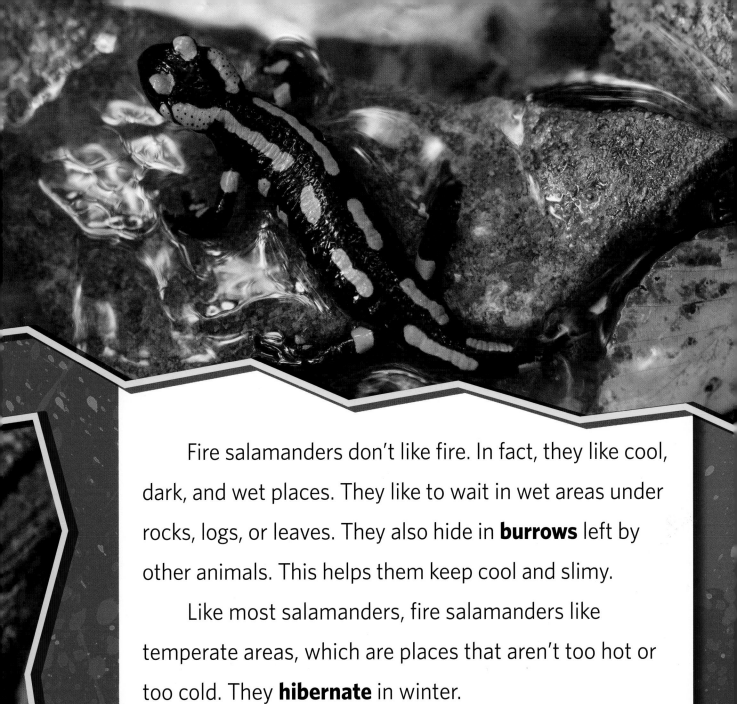

Fire salamanders don't like fire. In fact, they like cool, dark, and wet places. They like to wait in wet areas under rocks, logs, or leaves. They also hide in **burrows** left by other animals. This helps them keep cool and slimy.

Like most salamanders, fire salamanders like temperate areas, which are places that aren't too hot or too cold. They **hibernate** in winter.

Super Salamander Defenses

Fire salamanders have many great **defenses**. Their bright markings tell predators that they're **poisonous**. Predators don't want to bite into a poisonous meal! Fire salamanders can even spray their poison at predators.

Remember the axolotl salamander? Like the axolotl, other salamander species share their superpower. They can regrow their tail! If a predator surprises a fire salamander and bites its tail, the fire salamander can shed its tail and run away. Then, the fire salamander can grow another tail in its place. Salamanders can regrow their legs, too. Being able to regrow body parts is called regeneration.

FOOD FOR THOUGHT

Regeneration helps keep fire salamanders alive after a fight. Some fire salamanders live over 25 years in the wild!

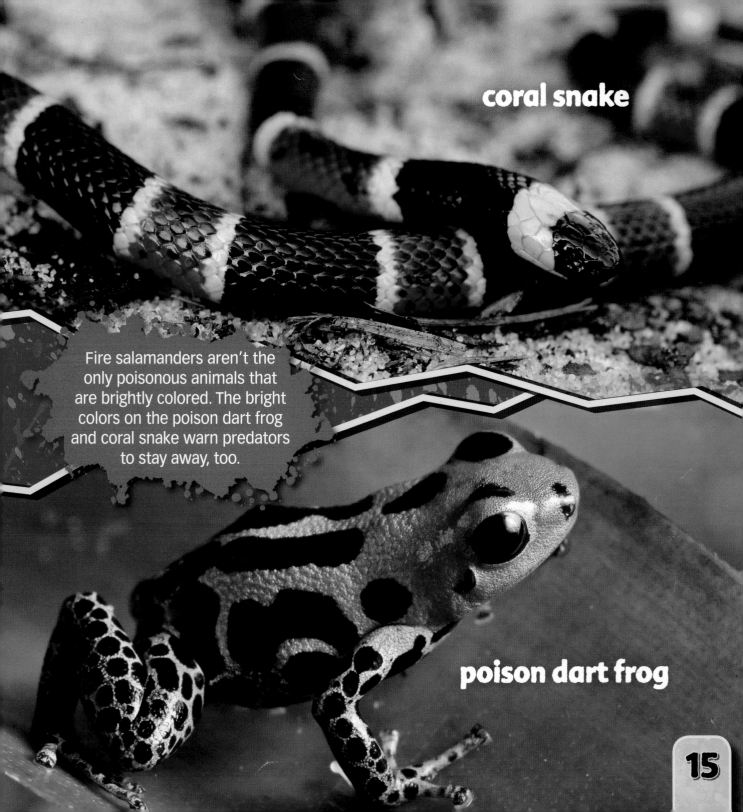

coral snake

Fire salamanders aren't the only poisonous animals that are brightly colored. The bright colors on the poison dart frog and coral snake warn predators to stay away, too.

poison dart frog

Quick Hunters

Fire salamanders are quick hunters. They often hide while hunting, so their **prey** is unaware. When a cricket trots along a fire salamander's path, the salamander strikes. It grabs the cricket with its sticky tongue and crunches it between its sharp teeth. Fire salamanders eat other **insects** and crunchy critters, such as millipedes, centipedes, and spiders. They also eat baby mice and small frogs.

Fire salamanders are known to eat other species of salamander. Even worse, they sometimes eat other fire salamanders. This happens especially when there are too many fire salamanders hanging around.

FOOD FOR THOUGHT

Fire salamanders give off poison through **glands** along their body.

Eating other fire salamanders keeps the population down, so there's more food to go around.

Baby Cannibals

Fire salamanders usually **mate** during the summer. After hibernating for the winter, the female usually gives birth in the spring. Like other amphibians, most salamanders lay eggs in water. However, fire salamanders are different. The female fire salamander carries the eggs inside of her as they grow. The female will give birth in water, such as a pond or deep puddle. After the baby salamanders are born, they're called tadpoles.

These little tadpoles look harmless, but don't be fooled. They're baby cannibals. When the female lays the tadpoles in water, some of them eat one another.

Tiger salamanders are nicer cannibals than fire salamanders. Tiger salamanders prefer to eat only tiger salamanders that are unrelated to them. That's good news for their families, at least!

tiger salamander tadpole

Metamorphosis

Fire salamander tadpoles don't look like fire salamanders at all. They have no legs, so they can't live on land. Instead, they use their tail to swim. Tadpoles breathe underwater with gills.

Over time, salamander tadpoles begin to change. They grow legs and teeth. They grow lungs that allow them to breathe air. This change from tadpole to adult is called metamorphosis. All salamanders and other amphibians go through metamorphosis. Metamorphosis in fire salamanders takes about three months. The adults are then ready to mate, which will make more baby cannibals.

Tadpoles are usually brown. As they become adults, their skin will turn black, and their colorful markings will appear.

Fire Salamanders and People

Some people keep fire salamanders as pets. Salamander owners need to give them cool, moist surroundings and many places to hide. Owners can feed fire salamanders worms and insects. While a fire salamander's poison won't kill you, it may hurt your skin a little.

Fire salamanders have more reason to be afraid of us, however. Fire salamanders live all over Europe. In some places, people are harming their homes by building on and polluting the area. Even though fire salamanders might sound scary, it's our duty to respect their surroundings and keep these cool cannibals safe.

Glossary

amphibian: An animal that spends the first part of its life in water and the rest on land.

burrow: A hole an animal digs in the ground for shelter.

defense: A feature of a living thing that helps keep it safe.

gland: A body part that produces something that helps with a bodily function.

hemisphere: One half of Earth.

hibernate: To spend the winter in a sleeplike state.

insect: A small creature that has three body parts and six legs and often has wings.

mate: To come together to make babies.

poisonous: Having poison, which is something that causes sickness or death.

prey: An animal hunted by other animals for food.

reptile: A cold-blooded animal with thin, dry pieces of skin called scales.

Index

A
amphibians, 4, 18, 20

B
burrows, 13

D
defenses, 14

E
Eastern Hemisphere, 10
eggs, 4, 18
estivation, 12

L
legs, 6, 8, 14, 20

M
markings, 4, 8, 14, 21
metamorphosis, 20

P
pets, 22
poison, 14, 15, 16, 22
predators, 4, 14, 15
prey, 16

R
regeneration, 14

S
species, 6, 7, 14, 16
subspecies, 10

T
tadpoles, 18, 20, 21
tail, 6, 8, 14, 20
teeth, 8, 16, 20
tiger salamander, 7, 19
tongue, 8, 16

Websites

Due to the changing nature of Internet links, PowerKids Press has developed an online list of websites related to the subject of this book. This site is updated regularly. Please use this link to access the list: www.powerkidslinks.com/ancan/fires